SAM MARTIN WENT TO PRISON

SAM MARTIN WENT TO PRISON

The Story of Conscientious Objection and Canadian Military Service

by William Janzen
and
Frances Greaser

Kindred Press

Winnipeg, MB Canada   Hillsboro, KS, US

Sam Martin Goes to Prison

Published simultaneously by Kindred Press, Winnipeg,
Manitoba R2L 2E5 and Kindred Press, Hillsboro,
Kansas 67063.

Typesetting and design by Publishing Services,
Winnipeg, MB
Cover design by TS Design, Winnipeg, MB

Printed in Canada by The Christian Press,
Winnipeg, MB

International Standard Book Number 0-921788-09-6

FOREWORD

We want to tell the story of Sam Martin's nineteen month imprisonment during World War II. It is not a pleasant story. It involves hardship, including three months of serious hardship in a military prison. But it also reveals the faith and courage of this young man, the support of his family, his church and his community, and the persevering friendship of a young woman.

We also want to provide a context for this story. For this reason we are telling, in Part II of this booklet, the history of conscientious objection to military service in Canada. This history, though marked by significant difficulties, is relatively positive. In World War II approximately 11,000 Canadian young men were given C.O. status. Most then followed orders and served under an alternative national service program. Sam Martin, though also willing to serve in this program, was among those whose applications for C.O. status were refused.

This broader history of conscientious objection is not the only context that is relevant to the Sam Martin story. Also to be noted is the enormous worldwide suffering and devastation that took place during World War II. Nearly seventeen million military people, including 44,000 Canadians, lost their lives during that war as did nearly nineteen million civilians.[1] Many more were injured. And countless others had to flee from their homes and homelands, never to return. Another 20–25 million people have died in smaller, more recent wars.

In one sense this terrible suffering makes Sam Martin's ordeal appear small. But all suffering is finally borne by individual people. And Sam Martin, in dealing with his situation, demonstrated exceptional courage, integrity, and faith. Those are timeless virtues and the primary reason for publishing this booklet is to convey them to the readers, particularly to young people. In addition this booklet may serve as a reminder, particularly at the fiftieth anniversary of World War II, that conscientious objection is part of the larger story of that war.

The process of preparing this booklet was quite involved. Frances Greaser, a long-time friend of the Martin family, was the first to write about Sam's experience. She shared her writing with Mennonite Central Committee Canada (MCCC) which indicated interest in carrying it further with the aim of publishing a booklet. I was then asked to do the additional work under the guidance of MCCC's Peace and Social Concerns office. We obtained files from several archives and comments from various people, including Mennonite historians and other C.O.s.

This broader counsel was instructive. Some individuals wanted us to acknowledge that there were sincere Christians, including Mennonites, who opted for a different course than the one followed by Sam Martin. Others, we found, had been personally inspired by Sam Martin to follow a similar course. One conscientious objector, D.J. Nikkel, wrote:

> The story of Sam Martin is very meaningful to me. It was his steadfastness and his living out of his faith that helped me to also make the same choice. Sam did not know at the time that his witness helped me. I too was rejected as a C.O. I returned my 'call' to the Military Authority and applied for postponement for which I never received an answer. After approximately six months, I was arrested. My sentence was thirty days in prison or a $30 fine, and then I was to be turned over to the Military Authorities. I ended up in Mewata Barracks, Calgary. The Sergeant who was responsible for me tried very hard to persuade me to go willingly. At the end of the conversation, he told me about a young man who refused to put on his uniform. He was in a stone cell, rationed to bread and water, and his health was being ruined. The Sergeant used this to try to intimidate me. However, the knowledge that someone else was willing to suffer for his faith gave me strength in my desire to live by my convictions. My decision to be willing to suffer was made. For this I give the Lord the honor. By nothing short of a miracle, I received a Permanent Discharge. This young man whom the Sergeant was telling me about turned out to be none other than Sam Martin. I later got to know him personally. He is a wonderful brother in the Lord.[2]

A question raised several times as we worked on this booklet is whether we were portraying the Canadian government in an excessively negative light. That is not our intent. There is no doubt that on the whole Canada was more respectful of conscientious objectors than most other countries involved in World War II. The vast majority of the Canadian young men who applied for C.O. status were given that status. Of those who were refused, some joined the military while others went to prison. At one point there were thirty C.O.s in jail at Headingley, Manitoba. But this was a civilian jail and most were assigned to work on the prison farm. According to one of these C.O.s, none suffered the kind of hardship experienced by Sam Martin during his three months in a military prison.[3]

However, at least one other C.O. did experience serious hardship. Frank Peters of Manitoba, who was imprisoned for two and one-half years, spent six months in military detention at the Fort Osborne Barracks. According to a brief report that he wrote in 1950 he was "heavily beaten with officers' sticks" when he arrived at the Barracks. Then he was put into a six-by-eight foot cell where he was kept on a diet of water and a pound of bread per day, not continuously, but for a total of 108 days over the six month period. Naturally, his physical condition deteriorated significantly. Only after he complained about severe back pains was he given a mattress and a blanket.[4]

Other people encountered problems of a different and less severe nature. A number of Manitoba Mennonites who were teaching in public schools had their teaching certificates temporarily concelled because of their C.O. stand.[5] And one person, John Goossen, was refused admission to Manitoba's medical school because he had spent some time in prison. The imprisonment had resulted from his C.O. stand.[6] Obviously, there are many stories waiting to be written up.

We are deeply grateful to Sam Martin for letting us publish his story. He did not seek publicity, neither as a hero nor as a martyr. Indeed he found it painful to tell certain parts of this story. Yet he graciously cooperated.

The contribution of others must also be acknowledged. Eleanor Dyck prepared the sketches for Part I. Lawrence Klippenstein provided photographs for Part II. Leona Penner, of MCCC's Peace and Social Concerns Office provided counsel and supervision. And Gilbert and susan Brandt of Kindred Press attended to various publication details.

William Janzen
Ottawa
February, 1990

About the Authors

Frances Greaser is a home-maker and nurse educator. She and her husband Lawrence live in Goshen, Indiana.

William Janzen is the Director of MCCC's Ottawa Office. He and his wife Marlene live in Ottawa, Canada

PART I
THE STORY OF
SAMUEL MARTIN

The court was formal and intimidating but Sam Martin answered clearly, "Your Honour, I will not be a soldier. I am a conscientious objector. Three times I have been told to join the military, but my answer is unchanged. The Scriptures, as I understand them, tell me not to kill."

The charge for which Sam had been brought before this court in Brooks, Alberta on April 19, 1944 was that he had refused to report for military training after being lawfully instructed to do so. The magistrate felt he had no choice but to find him "guilty." He sentenced Sam to thirty days in the Lethbridge provincial jail with instructions that he be "handed over" to the military thereafter.

Sam had strong convictions but these developments were deeply disturbing. Why was he refused when most other Mennonites were allowed to go into alternative service? How would he cope with prison life? What would the guards and the other inmates be like? Would he really be "handed over" to the military? What would happen then? And how would Beulah Good, with whom he had developed a special friendship at the Tofield Winter Bible School, feel about him in this situation?

How the Difficulties Began

Though Sam's imprisonment began on April 19, 1944, his encounter with the authorities dated back to December 28, 1942. (A list of significant dates in Sam Martin's story is provided on pages 35-37.)At that time, while employed in

his brother's garage in their home town of Duchess, Sam received his first call to report for military training. Sam responded by applying for conscientious objector (C.O.) status in the hope that he, like several of his brothers, would be sent to an alternative service work camp.

Seven weeks later he was called before the Mobilization Board in Edmonton. There the chairman, Judge Horace Harvey, questioned him.

"Do you attend church regularly?" he asked.

"Yes sir, I do," Sam replied. "I belong to the Duchess Mennonite Church. It is a peace church, and I belonged to it long before the war started."

"Have you ever been in trouble with the law?" the judge continued.

"No, except for one speeding ticket, " Sam answered.

To further explain his position Sam quoted various Scripture passages such as Matthew 5:39, 43 and 44; 26:52; John 18:36; 2 Corinthians 10:3,4; and James 4:1 and 2. However, the board was not sympathetic.It did not reveal the basis for itsdecision. Judge Harvey simply stated, "Martin, you have not convinced me."

The board's refusal to give Sam Martin C.O. status may have been influenced by the fact that many young Mennonites were serving in the army. Rev. B.B. Janz, a prominent Alberta Mennonite leader, had recently stated that almost one-half were going into the army. The Mobilization Board, according to chairman Harvey, had become "pretty well satisfied that if the young men are left to themselves there will be very little difficulty in getting them to take military training...as their conscientious objections are not their own but those of their parents or elders."

Although the board rejected Sam's C.O. application, it suggested that he could avoid military service if he immediately volunteered for the Merchant Marine. Workers in the Marine remained civilians and were not under the military but they were heavily involved with shipping military and other supplies across the Atlantic.

Sam did not see the Merchant Marine as an acceptable option either but a different factor now began to work in his favour. It was his value to the local farming community as a garage mechanic. When officials considered this, they gave him a year-long postponement, until March 31, 1944.

Sam was most grateful for this long postponement. He continued to work in the Duchess garage, owned by his brother Fred, where things were busy in the summer and fall of 1943. But the uncertainty of what might happen after the postponement ended weighed on his mind.

Nor was it a matter of not being tempted. Sam was an active young man. He enjoyed hunting, swimming and baseball and had often dreamt of becoming a pilot. Many of his friends had joined the Royal Canadian Air Force and some were now taking training flights over the town of Duchess. It looked exciting. Why could he not join them?

Early in March, 1944, before Sam's postponement came to an end, his father and his brother Fred wrote to ask that the postponement be extended. Among other things, they said that the community needed his mechanical services as much as ever. Their request was supported by a representative of the Alberta Federation of Agriculture.

However, now in an ominous turn of events, the postponement was not extended. Instead, Sam received a call to report for military training. Sam replied, stating respectfully, that he was a conscientious objector and would not serve in any military capacity but that he was willing to participate in the alternative service program.

A week later another notice came, warning that he would be arrested if he refused to comply. Sam wrote back again, explaining that the principles of his religion did not allow him to participate in any form of military service but that he was willing to accept alternative service.

When Sam did not report for training by the specified date, the Royal Canadian Mounted Police (R.C.M.P.) came to arrest him. This led to his appearance before the magistrate in Brooks on April 19, 1944, and to the thirty day sentence in the Lethbridge jail.

Thirty Days in a Provincial Jail

The prospect of thirty days in jail, with perhaps a worse fate thereafter, was worrisome but there was little that Sam could do. After the judge issued the sentence, an R.C.M.P. officer handcuffed Sam and led him across town to the train station. Since many people in Brooks knew him, Sam felt quite humiliated. At the station, he and the officer boarded a train for the 130 kilometre trip to Calgary. Sam remained shackled and under guard throughout.

In Calgary, Sam was held in the R.C.M.P. barracks for a few days as more prisoners were collected for the trip to the jail at Lethbridge. The R.C.M.P. photographed, fingerprinted and body-searched him to ensure that he was not smuggling anything. While in these barracks Sam helped with janitorial work. His cell-mate here was also a conscientious objector, a Doukhobor who refused not only military service but alternative service as well. For this he had already spent a year in the Lethbridge jail.

For the trip from Calgary to Lethbridge, Sam, like the other thirty prisoners on the train, was held in chains. On arrival at the large and imposing Lethbridge jail the prisoners were lined up and searched once more. Their hair was cut and their bodies were checked for lice. In addition there were rules about when to sleep, when to get up, when to eat, and what to do in the intervals. Moreover, all incoming and out-going mail would first be read by prison staff.

Fortunately, prisoners such as Sam who had short sentences and others who were nearing the end of their terms, were allowed to work outside on the prison farm. At first Sam was assigned to clean irrigation ditches with other prisoners but after one week, he was made responsible for the one-horse cart. This meant taking away the garbage, hauling ice blocks to the guards' houses, and doing other chores. It was a coveted position. He worked alone and often when he brought things to the guards' homes he was given tips such as baked goods and cigarettes. He gave the cigarettes to other prisoners.

To be responsible for the one-horse cart also meant

living in the Teamsters' Dormitory rather than in the cell-block. Here, there were fewer restrictions. The fifteen prisoners in this dormitory played cards and discussed many social issues. Sam was amazed at the diversity among the prisoners there.

Even though Sam was treated quite well in the Lethbridge jail, it was a lonely time, with worries about what might happen after the thirty days. Sam used much of his free time to read. Visits from outsiders were allowed but only through bars or a mesh screen. Also, they were preceded and followed by body searches. Still, the visits from his family, from his pastor, Rev. Clarence J. Ramer, and from Beulah Good, meant a lot to Sam.

While Sam was in the Lethbridge jail, his father and Rev. Ramer met with the Mobilization Board in Edmonton. Also, the Conference of Historic Peace Churches, with offices in Kitchener, Ontario, appealed to the federal government. They asked that Sam be given C.O. status and assigned to the alternative service program. The authorities refused. As for Sam, he was determined that if he was indeed "handed over" to the military he would not wear the uniform.

Twenty-Eight Days in a Military Prison

On May 13, 1944, even before his thirty day sentence had expired, it happened. Sam was "handed over" to the military. He was taken by military escort to the army's Mewata Barracks in Calgary and forcibly "enrolled" into the army. Physical examinations and intelligence tests followed and when the results of these were tabulated Sam was told that he could become an officer in the army. Sam replied that he was not interested.

Then, in what became a crucial test, he was issued a uniform. Sam's mind was made up. He would not wear it. When the officials saw this, they charged him with disobeying a lawful command. They took him before the Commanding Officer who sentenced him to twenty-eight days at Currie Barracks, a military prison thirty-five kilometres from Calgary.

These twenty-eight days were the beginning of a most difficult three months. Currie Barracks was a military prison for soldiers found guilty of desertion and disobedience. The treatment was much harsher than that in a civilian jail. Sam recalls, "Except for the Commander himself, Currie Barracks was run by the most sadistic people I have ever met."

When Sam arrived, in handcuffs, on May 25, the Regimental Sergeant Major showered him with bitter invectives, snarling, "You *will* wear a uniform! I am in charge here, and there has never been a person under my control whom I haven't been able to break! Take off your civilian clothes and put on an army uniform or go naked!"

"Sir," Sam quietly replied, "I refuse to serve in the army. I am a conscientious objector, and I will not wear the uniform." Out came another barrage of insults. Sam obediently took off all his clothes, except for his underwear, but he did not put on the uniform. Sam was then given an internal sentence: solitary confinement with a cyclical diet of three days on bread and water and three days on regular food. His cell, brightly lit up around the clock, had a bucket for a toilet but no bed, though he was given a few blankets for night-time. His civilian clothes were taken away so he was left virtually naked.

When the guards noticed that he still would not put on the uniform, they turned off the heat in his cell. Sam didn't react so they came into his cell, opened the window and ordered him to keep it open. When they left, Sam promptly shut the window. He was concerned about getting pneumonia. The guards then came in and opened the window again. Without comment, Sam closed it every time. After a number of efforts and much verbal abuse, the guards gave up and allowed him to keep the window closed. However they kept the heat for his cell turned off.

While this was happening, Sam's parents and his pastor were deeply concerned because they had not been given any information about Sam's whereabouts. Finally, his brother Fred came up with the idea of sending a telegram to Sam, addressed to the army, with a question about one aspect of the garage work that Sam had been doing. The army allowed Sam to see the telegram and to write a reply. In this way his family learned that he was alive and being held somewhere near Calgary.

Near the end of this sentence, late in June 1944, two

guards came and forcibly put a uniform on Sam and took him back to the army's Mewata Barracks in Calgary which served as a staging centre for sending recruits out to training camps.

Naturally, army officials there wanted to send Sam to a training camp too. However, at the first opportunity, though with much trepidation, Sam took off the uniform and put on army coveralls. Soon he was ordered to put the uniform back on but he replied as he had earlier, "I am a conscientious objector and I refuse to wear the army uniform."

Once more he was charged with disobeying a lawful command and told to wait for his next sentence. Though firm in his view, Sam had become weak and discouraged. The cyclical diet, the chill, the lack of clothing, the poor sleeping conditions, and the uncertainty about the future had taken a toll.

Another twenty-eight Days in Military Prison

To Sam's surprise, the Commanding Officer at Mewata Barracks, before whom he was brought for sentencing, was remarkably sympathetic now. He was concerned about Sam's weakened condition and had become impressed by his quiet demeanor and his willingness to cooperate wherever he could.

The commanding officer now told Sam: "I have gone to the trouble of reading about Mennonites and their non-participation in war. I have all kinds of sympathy for you and your position. The principles of pacifism have been born and bred into you. I doubt that you will ever be a soldier. But, and I regret to have to say this, I can do nothing for you. I have tried but I have met a stone wall of resistance from the authorities in Edmonton. By sentencing you again, I am only doing what I have to do."

And what was the sentence?— another twenty-eight days at Currie Barracks! Inwardly Sam shrank but there was nothing he could do. He was at the mercy of a system that knew little mercy. Upon arrival at Currie Barracks he again received a barrage of insults as well as a stiff internal sentence. For the first twenty-one days he would receive only bread and water for breakfast and supper, and a thick, tasteless porridge for lunch. Sam found the porridge so unpalatable that he rarely ate all of it. Soap and toilet paper were rationed too. He was allowed no clothes except his underwear. Of course, he could have put on the uniform at any time.

In addition he was placed in solitary confinement again. His cell, five feet wide and seven feet long, (213 cm x 152 cm) was totally bare except for a jar of drinking water and a bucket to be used as a toilet. At 10 p.m. each evening he was given three blankets to sleep on but these were taken away at 6 a.m. each morning. That left him cold in the daytime. Sometimes he would huddle in a corner with his arms around his knees for hours. Sometimes he would pace the floor, three steps forward and three steps backward, on and on.

Gradually Sam became despondent. He imagined that everyone had forgotten him, that no one cared. He still thought of Beulah Good continually but he felt he could not ask her to wait for him. He began to worry about permanent damage to his health.

In reality, Sam's family and church had not forgotten him. They prayed for him constantly. They also wrote letters. At the end of the twenty-one day period, a guard opened Sam's cell door, threw forty-five letters on the floor, and said gruffly, "You have fifteen minutes to read them."

Sam was so overwhelmed that he wept uncontrollably. He didn't know which letters to read first. As it turned out, he didn't have to decide. The guard left all the letters with him for a couple of days. As he read, joy and hope returned. His faith in God was renewed. Also, for the last week of this second twenty-eight day sentence he was allowed to eat regular food.

When Sam had completed the sentence late in July 1944, he was again taken to Mewata Barracks in Calgary where the army tried once more to have him begin military training. An official gave him a uniform but as in the past, Sam refused to put it on. As a result he was again charged with disobeying a lawful command. It seemed like an ongoing cycle.

Now the army arranged for court martial proceedings, complete with a prosecutor and a defender. Sam's pastor, Rev. Ramer, was allowed to serve as his character witness. Ramer argued that Sam was not simply being disobedient, but that he was following an accepted principle of his church, and that he should be given C.O. status and sent into the alternative service program. However the prosecutor emphasized that by not putting on the uniform Sam had disobeyed lawful army orders. The adjudicator agreed and sentenced him to ninety days at Currie Barracks.

This was a devastating blow. Instead of freedom, Sam had now received a sentence three times as long as the preceding ones. Many questions rushed to his mind. Would the officials at Currie Barracks again put him on a diet of bread and water, perhaps for the whole ninety days? Would they again put him in solitary confinement? Without clothing and without heat in his cell? How long would all this continue? When would his health break completely? Would he be "left to rot in his cell," as a guard had once said?

Did Sam Have Any Alternatives?

Though the prospects seemed extremely bleak, Sam remained firm in his conviction that he would not be a soldier. However, he did inquire whether he could be transferred to the U.S. since he was still a U.S. citizen. He had been born there and had come to Canada in infancy. After inquiring about the possibility of a transfer an officer came to discuss it with him but apparently the officer thought that Sam was too weak for a transfer and decided not to take the matter further.

Another idea involved service in the military's medical corps. In September of 1943, the government in Ottawa had agreed to let C.O.s serve in the military's Medical and Dental Corps while being fully assured that they would never have to bear arms. It had always been improbable that "medics" would have to bear arms but military officials had been unwilling to make it an absolute promise, lest they be needed in an emergency.

With this form of service now approved at the most senior government levels, some Mennonites went into it, arguing that this gave them an opportunity to save lives. However other Mennonites, including the group to which Sam Martin belonged, discouraged this form of service since it was still under military auspices and required some basic military training.

Understandably, when the authorities received numerous appeals on Sam's behalf they asked him whether he would consider this avenue of service in the Medical and Dental Corps. The records suggest that the officials raised it with him several times during his imprisonment in the spring and summer of 1944. However Sam, in a 1988 interview, stated that when he had asked for more information about this form of service, he had always understood that it was not absolutely non-combatant. "If I had understood it as absolutely non-combatant then, I believe, I would have accepted it," he said.

It appears, then, that as far as Sam could tell, there were no alternatives that he could pursue in good conscience. He would simply have to try to accept this suffering regardless of the consequences.

Back to the Military Prison

On August 16, 1944, Sam was taken back to Currie Barracks to begin serving the ninety-day sentence. As on the previous two occasions he received a lot of verbal abuse and was taken before the Commanding Officer for internal sentencing.

Strangely, this Commanding Officer, like the one at Mewata Barracks, had become sympathetic. He asked Sam whether he was willing to do certain kinds of work around the barracks, such as cleaning or kitchen work, so as to avoid the harsh punishment. Sam was most agreeable. He said, "I will cooperate in any way I can short of taking training to be a soldier. I am willing to wear army coveralls but not the uniform."

The Commanding Officer then proposed to the Regimental Sergeant Major that Sam be allowed to do this kind of work. However the Sergeant Major refused. He said, "It is regulations, Sir. Firstly, Martin disobeyed an order and must be punished for it. Secondly, every soldier within this custody is to be trained to be a better soldier. That would not happen under the arrangements you are proposing." Accordingly, Sam was once again sentenced to twenty-one days of solitary confinement on a bread and water diet.

Sam was almost overwhelmed. He could not make sense of this seemingly endless suffering. He knew of one young Mennonite whose application for C.O. status had been refused but who, after a few days of punitive treatment at Currie Barracks, had joined the army. Perhaps some officials were still hoping that he would do the same. One officer wrote that to maintain discipline in the military it was necessary to deal harshly with individuals who disobeyed.

Sometimes Sam felt that maybe he was too adamant in resisting the uniform. Was it not just another form of clothing, he would ask himself. But several Jehovah's Witness C.O.s at Currie Barracks told him that some of their C.O.s had accepted the uniform. They had then been taken to a military training camp but when they had refused to participate in the training exercises they, reportedly, had been beaten severely.

Sam also questioned his basic stance of refusing military service. But when he read certain Bible passages he concluded that he had no choice. In Matthew 5:43-44 Jesus said, "You have been told, 'Love your neighbour, hate your enemy.' But I tell you, love your enemies and pray for your persecutors so you can be children of your heavenly father." In Matthew 26:52 he stated, "Put your sword back into its place; for all who take the sword will perish by the sword." John 18:36 quoted Jesus as saying, "My Kingdom is not of this world: if my Kingdom were of this world then would my servants fight...." Sam also found comfort in such Bible passages as Job 13:15, "Though he slay me, yet will I trust in him."

At one point Sam's Bible was taken from him with the comment that it had already ruined him and that if they took it away then maybe, just maybe, he would forget about his ideas. Sam complained to the Orderly Officer who insisted that it be returned since it was illegal to remove it.

In spite of this small victory, the atmosphere at Currie Barracks was demoralizing. Inmates received little respect. There were innumerable insults. On one occasion an imprisoned soldier went on a hunger strike which he continued for nine days before the Commanding Officer came with a favourable response. Sam considered doing the same but felt it would be wrong to deliberately weaken his health further.

Sam was taken out of his cell each morning to have a shower. Three times a day he was taken to the kitchen to pick up three slices of bread. Every morning the prisoners had to scrub the floors of their cells and a small area in front of each cell. With these exceptions, Sam was always locked up in his cell.

Even though Sam's contact with other prisoners was very limited he did communicate with a sixteen year-old boy across the hall. This boy had lied about his age to get into the army. After induction, he had decided that he didn't like it so he had run away, only to be caught and sent to Currie Barracks.

Now Sam and this boy lay on their stomachs and whispered through the two-inch gaps under their cell doors. The youth had gone to Sunday school and knew some Bible stories so they talked a lot about the Bible. When the young man couldn't find particular verses to answer his questions, Sam looked them up for him and whispered back the page numbers.

An Unexpected Turn for the Better

While Sam was in prison, his family and his church continued to appeal to the authorities, asking that he be given C.O. status and sent into the alternative service program. Their efforts were supported by two non-Mennonite ministers who circulated a petition in an effort to demonstrate that the request had substantial non-Mennonite support. Approximately 140 non-Mennonites signed the petition, claiming that the principle of religious freedom required a favourable response.

These non-Mennonite ministers then gave the petition

to the Mennonite minister, Clarence Ramer, who on August 28 brought it to the Commanding Officer at Currie Barracks. This officer then brought it to Sam with the admiring comment: "Well, Martin, no one can say that you don't have friends."

The next day the Commanding Officer also allowed Rev. Ramer to visit Sam even though the Regimental Sergeant Major had insisted that Sam not receive any visitors during the twenty-one day punishment period. However, Ramer was told not to give any advice or information to Sam, only spiritual help. Also, all conversation had to be in the presence of a guard.

After some discussion with Sam, Rev. Ramer asked the guard if he could pray with Sam. Embarrassed, the guard walked away. Bowing his head, the pastor mentioned in his prayer all the community news he thought Sam would like to know, especially about Beulah Good who still cared for him.

The two non-Mennonite ministers also took the petition to the Mobilization Board in Edmonton. The Board still refused to give Sam C.O. status but the effort appeared to have an effect. Suddenly Sam was taken to the army doctor who, after conducting a physical examination, told the Commanding Officer: "You had better do something about Martin. His health is becoming precarious." The next day, on September 1, 1944, Sam was transferred back to the Lethbridge provincial jail to complete his ninety-day sentence.

For a total of forty-nine days Sam had been on a diet of bread and water, without clothes and without heat in his cell. He had been deeply chilled, become very weak and had lost quite a lot of weight. If Sam had collapsed or died, army officials would have been in trouble.

Back in a Civilian Jail

The Lethbridge prison was as immense as ever but to Sam it was a welcome sight. However, instead of being given time to recuperate he was immediately sent out to hoe sugar beets alongside other prisoners. But in his weakened condition Sam couldn't keep up. A guard berated him and demanded, in violent terms, that he keep up with the others. As he tried to do so, blood began to ooze from his weakened fingers. This made the hoe handle slippery and sticky. After hoeing only a few rows in the hot sun, Sam was exhausted.

Sam felt he had no choice but to refuse to do this work after lunch. Such a refusal would probably lead to three days of solitary confinement on bread and water in a cell dubbed "the black hole" because no light was allowed in, but Sam saw no alternative. He wondered whether he could

survive, though even the few hours out of doors had been somewhat rejuvenating.

After the noon meal, the Deputy Warden lined up the prisoners, called out their names, and assigned them to work gangs. When only Sam was left, the Deputy Warden turned and said, "Martin, move your stuff from the cellblock to the Teamsters Dormitory. I'm putting you back on the one-horse cart."

Sam was totally surprised. He could hardly believe the good news. Instead of a punishment, he was given a coveted position. He thought of the words in I Corinthians 10:13, "God keeps faith, and will not allow you to be tested above that which you can bear. When the test comes, he will provide a way out, by enabling you to sustain it."

One of Sam's first assignments on the cart was to haul away the noose which had been used in a hanging. Apparently the day before Sam arrived back at Lethbridge, three German prisoners of war had been hanged. They had been convicted of a murder inside their internment camp in Canada. The hangings had upset everyone in the prison. The Warden, who had to be present at hangings, later told Sam that he strongly opposed capital punishment and that the only way he could cope was to get thoroughly drunk afterwards.

The task of hauling away the noose made an unforgettable impression on Sam, but generally he enjoyed being back on the one-horse cart. He could work at his own speed and no one breathed down his neck with threats or shrill commands. He developed a pleasant routine. He would do his work, put his horse away and then go up into the hayloft in the barn where he had hollowed out a comfortable

place to read. He read books from the prison library, material brought there by the Salvation Army, and literature from his family and his church.

There were other experiences too. In one dormitory room there were two wires coming from an electrical box. For some reason, the light had been removed. When one of the prisoners learned that Sam had some house-wiring experience, he asked Sam if he would wire in a socket if one were provided.

"Stupidly," Sam says, "I agreed." That night, four prisoners, having obtained a socket and a bulb, went to that room and played poker all night.

The next day as Sam passed the Deputy Warden's office in his cart he was called in and asked, "Do you know anything about that light?"

"Yes sir, I wired it up," Sam replied.

"Where did you get it?" the Warden asked.

"Another prisoner gave it to me," Sam answered.

"Which prisoner?" the Warden asked.

With much hesitation, Sam said, "I can't tell you. My life would be in danger."

With that the Warden simply said: "Look, the next time we want any wiring done around here, we will call you. In the meantime, you just do the work we tell you."

Sam was relieved. He had expected severe punishment. Soon thereafter the Warden asked him to wire his house with better and more modern wiring.

In addition to the friendship with the Warden, the incident also increased the trust that the other prisoners had in Sam. They knew he would not squeal on them. Occasionally they asked him to take their concerns to the Warden.

A Brief Taste of Freedom

Late in October, 1944, as Sam completed his ninety-day sentence, he was taken from Lethbridge back to the army's Mewata Barracks in Calgary. Once there he asked the Commanding Officer for a weekend pass. To his surprise, it was quickly granted. Rev. Ramer then came and took him to his home in Duchess, where Beulah was waiting for him. Suddenly, the world seemed beautiful again!

This was also the Sunday for the semi-annual communion service of the Duchess Mennonite Church. Sam was deeply moved by the experience as he worshipped with his church family. He savored his mother's cooking and enjoyed the time with his family and with Beulah. He thought of asking her for a life commitment but he did not yet know if his health had been permanently damaged or what lay in store. Still, the weekend glimpse of natural beauty and the renewal of relationships was a healing experience. On Sunday evening, Sam's brother Joe and Beulah drove him back to the Mewata Barracks in Calgary.

An Eighteen Month Sentence

Once back at Mewata Barracks, Sam was again told to put on the army uniform and when he refused he was again charged with disobeying a lawful command. Now he was placed in the guard-house to await further developments.

While in detention, Sam discovered that the guard-house Sergeant was the one who had stolen his personal money when he had first been held there back in May. The Sergeant now begged Sam not to lay charges against him. However, the Commanding Officer, who wanted to send the Sergeant to jail, urged Sam to lay charges.

Sam responded, "I have just come from jail. I have no desire to put someone else there."

While Sam forgave the army Sergeant, the army was not about to let Sam go. Sam was again declared guilty of disobeying a lawful command but the sentencing procedures now were different. Sam was taken out to the parade square surrounded by hundreds of soldiers. Two soldiers escorted him to the centre of the square and left him standing there alone. Then a voice came over the loudspeaker for all to hear, "Sam Martin, sentenced to eighteen months in the Lethbridge Provincial Jail with hard labour."

Sam felt numb. Would the imprisonment never end? Fortunately, he would not be sent to the army's prison at Currie Barracks but eighteen months, with hard labour, albeit in a civilian jail, was a long time. But there was little that Sam could do.

When Sam arrived at the Lethbridge jail the Warden seemed unaware of the "hard labour" stipulation. Apparently it was not on the documents sent to the prison. However, Sam indicated to the Warden that he would prefer to do some work rather than just stay in a cell. This led to a wide range of activities.

At first he was assigned to a gang stacking hay. Later he was designated as the mechanic for the jail's twelve lawn mowers. While on this job, Sam noticed that the prisoners were deliberately damaging the mowers in order to get some rest time. Sam then urged the guard to give the prisoners rest breaks. The guard resented Sam's intervention but soon the prisoners began to receive the desired rest breaks.

Sam also repaired the Warden's car and much of the prison's farm machinery, including the threshing machine and the tractor. During harvest time he hauled grain from the threshing machine and was the first prisoner to be permitted to drive the prison truck into Lethbridge and do various outside errands. This could have aroused resentment from the other prisoners but it seemed that they all respected him.

When the farm manager, a man from the outside, was caught stealing, Sam and a somewhat older prisoner, were asked to jointly take on the job. Delighted at the promotion, Sam spent considerable time organizing and directing the prisoners in their assignments. After doing this throughout the summer of 1945, the Warden called Sam and his partner into his office and said, "Boys, we just want you to know that we are very pleased with the way you are running the farm. For the first time in its existence, this farm has made a profit."

There were personal friendships too. One was with another Mennonite whose case could not have been more different. This man wanted to be in the army. He had been declared a C.O. against his wishes and when he had been ordered to accept an alternative service assignment he had refused. This refusal had led to a one-year prison term. Later, after his release, this Mennonite enlisted in the army. In spite of their different orientations, the two Mennonites got along well during their time in prison. Several Jehovah's Witness C.O.s who had refused alternative service assignments for other reasons were also serving time in the Lethbridge jail.

Another of Sam's friends was a person who had been , sent to prison for armed robbery. He had become a Christian through the efforts of the Salvation Army and had

31

prayed that he would find another Christian in prison to whom he could relate. He soon met Sam and they developed a close relationship. Another prisoner with whom Sam became friends, later worked as a school teacher and a minister.

During the many months at this prison, Sam was allowed to receive mail and personal visits. Those from his family, his minister, and from Beulah were particularly meaningful.

Free At Last

Early in November of 1945, after serving two-thirds of his eighteen month sentence, Sam was called into the Warden's office and told that the balance of his prison sentence had been "remitted."

This was good news. His father, his minister, and the Kitchener-based Conference of Historic Peace Churches had made a number of appeals on his behalf both in Edmonton and in Ottawa.

However, the practical effect of this "remission" of his sentence was not immediately clear. Sam was still under the army's authority so he was simply transferred back to the army's Mewata Barracks in Calgary where the Commanding Officer exclaimed, "What am I supposed to do with you now?"

Since Canada's involvement in the war had ended months ago, the military training program had been largely dismantled. Sam then suggested that he be given a six month "industrial leave." This would allow him to go back to Duchess and work in his brother's garage. The Commanding Officer thought this was a great idea and issued the "leave" immediately.

At last Sam was a free man. He went to a hotel and phoned Beulah. She came to meet him and right there he asked her to marry him.

In mid-April 1946, near the end of the six month leave, Sam reported back to the army headquarters in Calgary where he was formally discharged. It was a normal honourable discharge but the document also carries the note, "Twenty-three months non-effective service."

In May of 1946, Sam and Beulah were married.

Sam Martin's Reflections, Forty-Five Years Later

In reflecting on his stand forty-five years later, Mr. Martin says, "I would encourage young people to stand up for their convictions and to remember that such decisions are not made in isolation. Parents and others suffer when an uncommon decision is made.

"I owe debts of gratitude to a lot of people, especially to my church. They not only worked to help in every way they could, but they kept in touch with me through hundreds of letters. It was their prayers that got me through. I always knew I had my home church behind me. Through this experience I received an understanding of what it means to be the church that has never left me. It is much more than an association of people. It is a body and when one member suffers, the whole body suffers. I am grateful also to the larger church family, particularly the people in Ontario whom I didn't even know but who worked on my behalf. I am indebted also to some government officials such as the prison warden at Lethbridge and others who became sympathetic to my situation.

"Of course, I owe a special debt of gratitude to Beulah who was very faithful in writing to me and visiting me when she could and encouraging me in every way. There is no way in which I can adequately express my gratitude to her for the way she stayed with me in my time of trouble, especially since she didn't know when I would get out.

"I also owe an enormous debt to my pastor, C.J. Ramer. I doubt whether any minister ever deserved more gratitude and admiration than he. He constantly supported me in every way he could. He frequently travelled hundreds of miles to plead for me, even though sometimes he was scoffed at, ignored, and verbally abused. He made an indelible impression on me. He spent a lot of time working on my case even if he had a lot of other work to do. He certainly became a spiritual father to me, and I can't say enough about his help.

"My parents also suffered with me. While my father made frequent pleas to the Board, my mother was praying and worrying about me. Thoughts of praying parents and family got me through many rough times. I am extremely grateful for the care and support they and all my family gave me. Young people need to realize how the decisions they make affect their parents and those they love. Although I don't regret my decision, I am sorry that my parents had to suffer so much anguish in their concern for me. But I will always be grateful for their support and love."

- - - - - - - - - - - - - - - - -

The on-going Christian commitment of Sam and Beulah is evident in the substantial contribution that they have made to the church in the following decades. Both served the Duchess Mennonite Church in numerous capacities. In 1965, Sam was elected to be a minister in that church. Also, for nearly fifteen years he served as a minister for the province-wide conference of churches.

SIGNIFICANT DATES IN SAM MARTIN'S STORY

December 17, 1922   Sam Martin's date of birth.

September 8, 1939   Canada declared war.

June 18, 1940   Parliament passed the conscription law

August 19–21, 1940   National registration for all men and women over sixteen.

December 28, 1942   Sam's first call to report for military training.

February 20, 1943   Sam appeared before the Mobilization Board in Edmonton which then refused his application for conscientious objector status. However, officials gave him a long postponement until March 31, 1944.

March 1, 1944   Sam's father and his employer applied for an extension of the postponement. This was refused.

March 23, 1944   Sam was called to report for military training by April 5.

March 27, 1944   Sam wrote back explaining that he would not go.

March 30, 1944   Sam's call was returned, with a warning that he would be arrested if he refused.

April 4, 1944   Sam wrote back again, explaining that he would not go.

April 19, 1944   Sam was taken before the magistrate in Brooks, Alberta who gave him his first sentence: Thirty days in the

	provincial jail in Lethbridge.
May 13, 1944	Sam was taken to the army's Mewata Barracks in Calgary and forcibly "enrolled" into the army.
May 24, 1944	Sam, who refused to put on the uniform, was charged with disobeying a lawful command and given his second sentence: Twenty-eight days in the military prison known as Currie Barracks.
June 23, 1944	Sam, who again refused to put on the uniform, was charged once more with disobeying a lawful command and given his third sentence: Another twenty-eight days at Currie Barracks.
July 21, 1944	Sam again refused to put on the uniform. This led,on July 29, to court martial proceedings and to his fourth sentence: Ninety days at Currie Barracks.
September 1, 1944	Following an examination by an army doctor, Sam was transferred back to the Lethbridge provincial jail to complete his ninety-day sentence.
Late October, 1944	Sam was taken back to Mewata Barracks, where he again refused to put on the uniform. This led to his fifth sentence: Eighteen months at the Lethbridge provincial jail.
May 8, 1945	Canada ceased to be at war in Europe. In the Pacific region the Canadian war effort ceased on September 1, 1945.
October 23, 1945	The remainder of Sam's prison sentence was "remitted." Soon

	thereafter he was taken back to the army's Mewata Barracks.
November 8, 1945	Army officials gave Sam an "industrial leave." He then went back to work in his brother's garage in Duchess, Alberta.
April 12, 1946	Sam was formally discharged from the army.
May 22, 1946	Sam Martin and Beulah Good were married.

PART II
THE BROADER
STORY OF
CONSCIENTIOUS
OBJECTION IN
CANADA

Samuel Martin's story raises many questions. What were the legal provisions for conscientious objection to military service? What was the alternative service program all about? What were the non-combatant forms of military service? What is the broader story of conscientious objection in Canada?

Early History

That broader story has a long and complex history.[1] In 1793, the Militia Act passed by the Assembly of Upper Canada, included a promise of exemption for Mennonites, Tunkers (now called Brethren in Christ) and Quakers. They had asked for an exemption and the government readily agreed. It wanted to attract more settlers from these groups still living in Pennsylvania. The exemption provision meant that the men did not have to participate in the brief militia exercises held each year. It also spared them from combat duty in the War of 1812, though some were required to provide transport service, using their own horses. Also, until 1849 they had to pay a supplementary tax.

A second promise of exemption was made in 1873 to encourage Mennonites from Russia to settle in Manitoba. This promise, given by the federal cabinet in the form of an Order-in-Council, was based on an 1868 revision of the early Militia Act. The 1873 Order-in-Council promised an

A group of Russian Mennonite men are marching off to work at a forest camp located at Alt-Berdyansk, in south Russia.
(From *That There be Peace*, p. 19)

"entire exemption" and a related Order-in-Council referred to "the fullest assurances of absolute immunity from military service." This was important to these Mennonites. One reason why they wanted to leave Russia was that the government there had taken steps to require a national service, even if not military service.

In spite of these promises, there were serious difficulties in World War I.[2] The Military Service Act of 1917 unintentionally divided Mennonites into two categories. Those Mennonites covered by the 1873 Order-in-Council, as well as the Doukhobors covered by a similar 1898 Order-in-Council, were "excepted" from the Act and as such had no duty to perform there under. But those Mennonites, Brethren in Christ and Quakers in Ontario, whose older promise of exemption had provided the basis for the Orders-in-Council of 1873 and 1898, had to cope with a provision which only exempted those who: a) had a personal conscientious belief against undertaking combatant service; and b) belonged to a religion which the government recognized as prohibiting such service. Obviously this meant that they could still be called up for non-combatant service.

The "incompleteness" of this exemption was of serious concern to Ontario churches. Fortunately, the 1917 Act also allowed people to be exempted if their labour was badly needed elsewhere. Since most Mennonites and Brethren in Christ were farming people and since the production of food was a national priority, many were exempted on this basis. But then, in April 1918, seven months before World War I ended, all exemptions for people in certain age categories were cancelled including the partial exemptions granted on grounds of conscience. This cancellation raised deep concerns. Bishop S.F. Coffman and other Ontario church leaders made strong appeals. As a result an arrangement was worked out whereby the young men from these groups would enlist but military leaders would then grant them "leaves of absence." It was not a comfortable procedure but it worked, though some young Mennonites were detained in military camps and prisons for brief periods. The story of the imprisonment of Ernest J. Swalm, who later became a Brethren in Christ bishop, was subsequently published.[3]

In western Canada there were problems too. The "exception" based on the Order-in-Council of 1873 was interpreted in increasingly narrow ways. Near the end of the war this Order-in-Council was said to cover only those Mennonites who had come from Russia to Manitoba in the 1870s, not those who had come from the United States and Europe in the 1890s and early 1900s even though these had been told, at the time of their immigration, that that Order covered them too. Also, as in Ontario, there was debate about the eligibility of the young men who had not yet formally joined the church. Were they Mennonites? Were they covered by the law? And if Mennonite bishops were to certify who was a Mennonite and who was not, might the bishops misuse their authority?

While responding to these technical problems, deeper questions also arose. Some people wondered how Mennonites could, in good conscience, expect others to sacrifice their lives while they were reaping benefits from those sacrifices. Bishop David Toews from Saskatchewan responded to this in one letter, stating:

> We do not require anyone to shed his blood for us. We would rather die ourselves or languish in prison or leave our homes and settle again in some wilderness as our forebears have done, than to require a sacrifice of any kind by anyone on our behalf[4]

Even more difficult than the Mennonite situation were the problems facing individuals from religious groups which were not formally recognized as having a basic teaching against military service. According to the law they could not get C.O. status. Approximately 130 such individuals were imprisoned. Some Jehovah's Witnesses, then known as International Bible Students, were treated brutally. One Pentecostal conscientious objector, David Wells, died three weeks after being sent to a Manitoba prison. There was strong speculation that his death was the result of torture.[5] His death brought protests from the press, certain church leaders, trade unions, and even from other soldiers.

While the difficulties in getting exempted from military service can be attributed to inadequate laws, the underlying social climate must also be noted. In World War I, nearly 750,000 Canadians served in the armed forces. Of these,

66,700 died and many more were wounded. Since Canada's total population was only eight million at that time and since Quebecers were seriously under-represented in the military, people in other parts of Canada were intensely involved. They felt their sacrifice keenly. This makes it understandable that the non-participation of Mennonites and others aroused a certain resentment. For Mennonites the situation was complicated further by the fact that they spoke German, the language of the enemy, and that some of them prospered because of the war-time economy. The resentment became so strong that for a brief period after World War I, the federal government banned further Mennonite immigration.

Anticipating World War II

When the possibility of another great war appeared, the situation of Canadian Mennonites included a major new element. Approximately 21,000 Mennonites had come to Canada from Russia in the 1920s[6] They brought with them a slightly different experience, having long sponsored an alternative national service program in Russia. In 1881, following new governmental policies, their young men had been sent out on forestry assignments. When World War I came, they also undertook extensive medical corps work alongside the Russian military. They had "complete hospital units, including stretcher bearers who gathered the wounded on the battlefield, complete hospital trains transporting them back to hospitals at Ekaterinoslov and Moscow, also fully manned by Mennonites." About 8,000 Mennonites served in the medical corps while 4,000 continued in forestry work. Some 120 of those in the medical corps lost their lives in the war. As in forestry work, virtually the entire cost was carried by the Mennonite communities.

When these Mennonites arrived in Canada in the 1920s they inquired whether they, like other Mennonites, would be exempted from military service. The responses were reassuring but not entirely clear. In 1924 a senior Justice Department official wrote that the Order-in-Council of 1873, while still valid for the descendants of those who immigrated at that time, would not cover those immigrating now, half-a-century later. The newcomers, he stated, would be covered by the provision in the Militia Act which exempted "Persons who from the doctrines of their religion are averse to bearing arms or rendering personal military service." What did this mean? Was it an exemption from combatant service only? In 1935, another senior official wrote that all Mennonites were eligible for exemption on the same

World War II alternatives service workers in Kananaskis Valley, Alberta, skidding logs, sawing mine props, 30 degrees below, men warming up at fire. (Photo: H.R. Baerg,in *That There be Peace,* **p.34)**

basis, namely that provided in the Militia Act.

In addition to seeking legal assurances, some Mennonite leaders recognized that they might also need to respond to certain social pressures. Specifically, they would have to demonstrate that they too, were willing to serve and to sacrifice, albeit in a different manner. This concern, and the desire for a more unified approach, led Bishop David Toews to invite a broad range of Mennonite leaders to a meeting in May, 1939. Hutterites too were represented. In the discussions it quickly became clear that while all wanted exemption from military service they were not agreed on the question of alternative service. The "Russländer Mennonites," meaning those who had come from Russia in the 1920s, favoured an alternative service, somewhat along the lines of their programs in Russia. However, the "Kanadier Mennonites," meaning those who had come from Russia in the 1870s, saw it as a compromise.[7] They were not categorically opposed, but they did not want to offer such a service to the government. The

"Swiss Mennonites," concentrated in Ontario, (many had come from Switzerland via Pennsylvania), were also hesitant.[8]

The inability to agree on the alternative service question was not crucial in the spring of 1939. Canada was not yet conscripting anyone. Indeed, the country was still not at war. When the fighting began in Europe, all the Mennonite groups increased their international relief work. In Ontario, the Non-Resistant Relief Organization, set up in World War I, was revitalized and in the West, other committees were set up. Large amounts of food and clothing were gathered and sent overseas together with the necessary personnel. Much of this relief work was done in association with the Mennonite Central Committee, based in Akron, Pennsylvania.

Alternative service workers on the way to work in Riding Mountain National Park. (Photo: J.K. Reimer in *That There be Peace*, p.27.)

Cutting burned trees on Vancouver Island.(Photo: Ben Hildebrand in *That There be Peace*, p.43)

Formulating Laws For World War II

On September 8, 1939, Canada declared war. Great Britain and France had declared war a few days earlier. At first Canada relied on volunteer enlistments but in June, 1940, a conscription law, formally known as the National Resources Mobilization Act, was passed. However, because of concerns about Quebec, this law authorized conscription only for home defense. The intent was to create a pool of trained soldiers, many of whom would then volunteer for overseas service. In mid-August 1940 there was a national registration aimed at all men and women over sixteen. Later in August the government announced the National War Services Regulations, providing details about how the conscription process, including exemptions for C.O.s, would operate.

As in World War I, the exemption provisions had two categories. One category referred to the descendants of Mennonites and Doukhobors who had immigrated to Canada pursuant to the Orders-in-Council of 1873 and 1898. The other category referred to C.O.s, defined as individuals who: a) had a conscientious objection, meaning a personal belief against bearing arms or undertaking combatant service; and b) belonged to a religious denomination whose articles of faith prohibited such service. The Regulations also stated that people exempted from military service, in either of these two categories, could be compelled to render a non-combatant service under military or civilian auspices.

With the announcement of these Regulations in August 1940, a number of Mennonite leaders felt that they now had to make up their minds on the question of alternative service. In Ontario, Mennonites had become more sympathetic to such a service, partly because of the clear interest of the Quakers with whom they were now associated in the new Conference of Historic Peace Churches (CHPC). Accordingly, in September, 1940 the Ontario based CHPC sent a delegation to Ottawa not only to discuss procedures whereby individuals could obtain C.O. status but also to express their desire "to make some positive contribution to the country's welfare, provided this could take the form of constructive civilian work under civilian control."

In contrast, in western Canada, the reluctance of the "Kanadier Mennonites" to offer an alternative service increased, partly because the new governmental Regulations referred to their historic Order-in-Council. This, supplemented by a September meeting with representatives of the National War Services Board for Manitoba, led them to believe that they would receive a "complete exemption" meaning an exemption from both military service and alternative service. Accordingly, they did not wish to offer an alternative service to the government, though they would certainly continue to support international relief work.

The other Mennonites in western Canada, particularly the "Russländer" and those who had immigrated from the U.S. and Europe around the turn of the century, now joined with the CHPC in Ontario in proposing an alternative service program to the government. Meeting in Ottawa in November, 1940 their leaders proposed that the service be "of an agricultural or forestry nature combining, if pos-

Raking hay for Buffalo feed in Alberta. (Photo: P.K. Wiebe, in
*That There be Peace***, p. 24, P.K.Wiebe)**

sible, reforestation, setting up of nurseries as needed, land reclamation and farm improvements." They also asked that this work "be done on government owned land in order that the benefit from the labour expended should accrue to the country as a whole." They emphasized that the work would have to be under civilian control. They also asked that the men be organized in groups so as to facilitate spiritual supervision.

Though the Meenonite proposal was substantial , the government's initial response was not positive. Officials felt that setting up a separate service program would be too costly and complex and that only a few young men would be interested. They asked the delegates to consider noncombatant service under the control of the military, such as first-aid to the wounded or maintenance work at military camps, stating that for the latter the men would not need to wear a uniform. One delegate, Rev. B.B. Janz, indicated a willingness to consider non-combatant medical service on the front lines. Janz, who was familiar with the Russian experience, felt that this would clearly demonstrate the desire of the Mennonites to not only refrain from taking life but to be active in saving it. Also, coming from Alberta, Janz knew the social pressure since two Alberta Mennonite churches had been burned down in June, 1940. Other Russländer leaders, though sympathetic, continued to press for a civilian program so as not to further alienate the other Mennonite groups. However, the officials continued to resist the idea. At one point, Major-General L.R. Lafleche asked impatiently, "What would you do if we shoot you?" To this Jacob H. Janzen responded forcefully,

> Listen, Major-General, I want to tell you something. You can't scare us like that. I've looked down too many rifle barrels in my time to be scared in that way. This thing is in our blood for 400 years and you can't take it away from us like you'd crack a piece of kindling over your knee. I was before a firing squad twice. We believe in this.[9]

Soon thereafter the government agreed to set up a civilian alternative service program. However, this required numerous practical arrangements so it was June, 1941, before the first 1,000 men who had been given C.O. status, were sent out on alternative service assignments. Many of those in the west were sent to national parks at Banff, Jasper, Prince Albert, and Riding Mountain, where they cleared forests of dead timber, built trails and roads to fight forest fires more effectively, planted trees, constructed drainage facilities, etc. Those in Ontario were sent to a camp eighty miles north of Sault Ste. Marie to clear the way for what would become the Trans-Canada Highway.[10] The assignments were to last four months, a time equal to the military training period required of recruits.

Many Mennonite leaders were pleased when the alter-

Ontario men at a camp near Campbell River (Photo: Ben Hildebrand, in *That There be Peace*, p. 45.)

native service workers were finally sent out. Now the larger society could be shown that Mennonites too were willing to serve. Also, since the program was of a civilian nature, it was acceptable to virtually all Mennonites. Even the Kanadier Mennonites participated, having been told in a February 1941 trip to Ottawa that a "complete" exemption from all national service was no longer possible.

Difficulties with Military Exemption

While the commencement of alternative service work was a major step forward, there were problems with getting exemptions from military service. These problems revolved around two issues. One was the question of non-combatant service under military auspices. In a sense this form of service was in between regular military service and civilian alternative service so it is understandable that National War Services Boards in several provinces tried to persuade the young Mennonites to accept this. Some young men agreed, though church leaders did not endorse noncombatant military service.

The other problem area involved the personal appearances before the Boards. All Mennonite groups had wanted to avoid these. They had asked that their young men be exempted from military service on the basis of lists prepared by church leaders. In Ontario this became the practice. But in the prairie provinces, personal appearances were required, even from the Kanadier who, arguably, could claim a collective exemption on the basis of the 1873 Order-in-Council.

The personal appearances varied. Many young men had their C.O. applications approved after only a few questions. But board members and representatives of the military could be hard and unsympathetic. Also, a young man was not allowed to have a lawyer or a minister to help him explain his views. As a result, there were occasions when the men were strongly pressured to consider regular military service or at least noncombatant military service

In Manitoba the Board Chairman, Judge J.E. Adamson, believed that many young Mennonites, if left to themselves, would join the military, as in fact many did. Accordingly, he urged the church leaders not to try to influence their men. He also turned down a number of those who asked for exemption. When these then refused to report for military training they were prosecuted and some were jailed. Complete figures are not available but at least thirty Manitoba Mennonites spent some time in prison. Some were sentenced to twelve months with hard labour though in a number of cases, these sentences were eased after several months.

In Saskatchewan, there were serious difficulties too. Board chairman, J.F.L. Embury was critical of Mennonites. In one letter, following an encounter with some young men from Hepburn, perhaps from the Mennonite Brethren Bible school there, he wrote:

> Some schools have been carrying on all across this Province and Alberta and Manitoba openly teaching High German, and turning out students intended to be preachers, some of whom, openly in effect, say they are not interested if Hitler wins this War or not— as they will leave it to Providence...it is to us nothing more or less than an utterly traitorous doctrine which has not even the remotest connection with religious doctrine...
>
> ...some of our public Schools have been used to instill into the minds of the young people at a tender age that they should never engage in war, regardless of the circumstances. How then is it possible when this kind of thing goes on, to create a nation able to defend itself?...[11]

Embury was reluctant about approving applications for exemption. At one hearing of 126 applicants in December, 1941, seventy were refused. This treatment, which seemed to be less focused on the Kanadier Mennonites than on others, was of great concern to the Saskatchewan leader, David Toews. He felt that the board had often made up its mind to reject applications before the hearings took place. In the summer of 1942, Toews wrote to senior Ottawa officials, stating:

> Our boys are not recognized as Mennonites nor as conscientious objectors. I claim that ministers who have known the boys from their youth on know more about their convictions than a biased Board could know after they have examined them for five or ten minutes.

...A young Mennonite...came before the Board and one of the questions was: "Did you go to school?" Answer: "Yes". Question: "Did you ever have a scrap in school?" Answer: "Yes." — "Well, you are not a conscientious objector, your application is not accepted, get out!!!"

Another boy came before the Board. "Are you a Mennonite and a conscientious objector?" Answer: "Yes." — "Why is it that you are asking for postponement?" Answer: "Besides being a Mennonite and a conscientious objector, I am a farmer and I am the only one working on the farm." Answer: "I do not care a hoot about your farm, we want you, your application is not accepted, get out!!!"[12]

In another letter Toews wrote:

...If only some of the young men,...were not recognized as conscientious objectors, I do not think that I would have taken the liberty to write to you, but if almost all of our young men are not given recognition as having conscientious scruples about military service, I believe some consideration should be given to this fact.[13]

In the fall of 1942, David Toews from Saskatchewan, and C.F. Klassen from Manitoba, travelled to Ottawa and made a lengthy appeal. Their statement described the problems in detail and concluded as follows:

Conditions are becoming unbearable in Manitoba and Saskatchewan....Is it just to put men in gaol who are ready and willing to do the other work provided by our Government? Why is the testimony of the ministers given no consideration? Why are Mennonites examined and cross-examined by lawyers as though there is an attempt to hide the truth? Have we not established a reputation for honesty and truthfulness?

We humbly submit, that justice demands that the situation be changed so that there is a possibility of an appeal for those who are refused recognition as Mennonites or conscientious objectors. (Emphasis in the original.)[14]

While the church leaders made strong appeals, the problems had additional dimensions. The Boards cited instances of young men who had made strong pleas for C.O. status but who, soon after being given that status, had enlisted in the army voluntarily. This made it hard for the Boards to assess whether a given man's objections was really "conscientious" and sincere.[15] Judge Adamson said that the only way to ensure that no sincere C.O. was ever rejected would be to approve every application. But if this were done then many insincere applicants would also be approved, he felt. As for a system whereby the decisions of the Boards could be appealed, this idea had the support of two prominent Saskatchewan politicians, John Diefenbaker and T.C. Douglas, but the government felt that it would complicate and slow down the recruitment effort too much. However the government did, on occasion, urge the Boards to "rehear" cases. In this way some injustices were corrected.

If some of the Boards were not sympathetic, neither were all elements in the public. There was a certain antipathy toward C.O.s. One reason for this was the government's slowness, early in the war, in setting up alternative service work projects. As a result many young men who had been granted C.O. status were not called up for alternative service work. They just continued with their normal lives and did not serve or sacrifice at all. Fortunately, this changed in 1942 and 1943.

Diversification in alternative service

Alongside the difficulties in obtaining exemption from military service there was, by 1942, a growing recognition that the alternative service workers could relieve the increasing labour shortage. The men were recognized as hard-working, reliable, orderly, and decent. Farm associations, businesses, railway companies and others, became interested in their services. One thousand C.O.s were sent to the British Columbia Forestry Service in 1942 to fight forest fires which, it was feared, might be started as sabotage action following the Japanese attack on Pearl Harbour in December, 1941.

Also in 1942, the government transferred the alternative service program from the Department of National War Services to the Department of Labour. Soon, more alternative service workers were called up and instead of four month assignments they were now sent out for the duration of the war. But this had other effects. It deepened concerns about family contact, spiritual supervision, romantic relationships, etc. It also created a labour shortage on Mennonite farms at a time when the government wanted to increase agricultural production. Provisions were then made for farm "leaves," for those already in the alternative service camps, and for farm "postponements" for those not yet called up. But these "leaves" and "postponements" were not easily obtained. A few Mennonites played "hooky."

In 1943, there was a more extensive diversification with the result that alternative service workers, who now numbered many thousands, were sent to industries, food-processing plants, hospitals, farms, and various other assignments. A majority of the Mennonites were now assigned to farms at least for the summer. In winter many were sent back to lumber camps and other activities. All alternative service workers now had to sign "contracts" stipulating that they could receive a regular salary but that they had to give all but a portion of it to the Red Cross. Alongside this more elaborate alternative service program, the government, in December, 1943, authorized military officials to discharge men who had been conscripted but who continued to insist that they were C.O.s. After discharging them from the military they could then go into the alternative service program. Why Sam Martin was not discharged on this basis is not known.

Alternative service worker with a patient at the St. Boniface Hospital in Winnipeg. (Photo: David Schroeder, in *That There be Peace*, p. 49.)

Alternative service worker at the St. Boniface Hospital. (*Photo: David Schroeder, in That There be Peace*, p. 52.)

Another noteworthy development is that in September, 1943, the government agreed to allow C.O.s to serve in the military's medical corps with the complete assurance that they would never have to bear arms. But this assurance applied only to individuals serving in the regular medical corps. Mennonites were still not allowed to have their own medical corps unit as they had had in Russia. Still, a number of Russländer Mennonites supported this avenue of service. It meant that they would be active in saving lives. It might also attract some of the young men now going into regular military service.

Other Mennonites, however, opposed this service in the military's medical corps. The CHPC of Ontario with which Sam Martin's Alberta church was connected, and the Kanadier Mennonites in the west, now reaffirmed their earlier views that non-combatant service under military auspices, even in the medical corps, was not acceptable. By the end of the war, 227 men had taken up this form of "restricted service." At least one of these, Isaak Lehn from Leamington, was killed during the allied invasion of Europe.[16]

Non-Mennonite Groups

Not all of the C.O.s exempted from military service were from church groups with long held teachings against such service. A few were United Church people, Anglicans, Baptists, Pentecostals, Plymouth Brethren, Seventh Day Adventists, Jehovah's Witnesses, and others. At first the Regulations stated that only people belonging to church groups which held non-participation in military service as a basic principle were eligible for exemption. But in December, 1940 it was broadened so that people belonging to any religious body were eligible. By 1942, this was broadened further so that even people who did not belong to any religious body could go before a board and argue that they had a "conscientious objection" to military service.

Some individuals from these other church groups, like some Mennonites, were well-educated and had long argued that diversification in the alternative service program was needed to "enable each person to make the largest possible contribution to the good of Canada and of all mankind."

Eventually, one group of twenty—mainly Mennonites and United Church people—were allowed to enlist and serve in the Firefighting Corps in England. Another group of twenty, organized largely by the Quakers and the missionary doctor, Robert B. McClure, who years later became moderator of the United Church, went to China to serve with a Friends Ambulance Unit. [17]

In a very different way, the diversification also affected the Doukhobors who had been promised military exemption with an 1898 Order-in-Council. They had tended to remain distant from governments. In the national registration of 1940 they had been allowed, after persistent requests, to register their own people—11,000 of them, not counting 2,000 Sons of Freedom Doukhobors. Most had not been compelled to appear before the Boards to gain exemption from military service. In 1941 some Saskatchewan Doukhobors were called up for alternative service work, but only a portion responded. The government then sent ninety-two of those who refused, to prison for a four month period. Thereafter, the government left virtually all of them, both in Saskatchewan and in British Columbia undisturbed in their regular work.

With the 1943 diversification, officials made further efforts to involve the Doukhobors. At first they were not successful. But the Doukhobors did not want to appear stubborn. A British Columbia Doukhobor statement said:

> Our refusal of medical examination and alternative service does not mean we won't do anything for the country we live in, or rather that we are not doing anything nor have we any idea to fight the Government. It would be a most unfortunate day for us to see jails filled with Doukhobors, where they would become a burden upon the government instead of an asset through their working capacity. However...the Doukhobors will abide by their principles of religion notwithstanding any consequences. [18]

If the Doukhobors could get away without participating in the alternative service program, then they were, arguably, outside the law. This was of concern to officials. There was talk of sending them to internment camps. However, the R.C.M.P. opposed this, stating:

the majority, if not all, are already engaged in such work as farming, mining, dam construction, logging and railway maintenance, which work is generally regarded as being in the national interest.... If it is intended...to compel them to do what they are already doing voluntarily, these religious fanatics will, it is believed, continue to protest by all possible means.[19]

The R.C.M.P. argued further that efforts to force them into formal compliance with the alternative service program would require too many officers. After considering various options, officials decided, in the fall of 1944, to approach them in a non-pressuring manner to have them direct a portion of their monthly earnings to the Red Cross even without an official "alternative service contract." Most, except the Sons of Freedom, agreed to do this.

Jehovah's Witnesses, operating from their own theological framework, also claimed C.O. status but they did not feel that they should render an alternative service. This resulted in many complications.[20]

Conclusion

Clearly, there were significant differences among those who on religious or conscientious grounds objected to regular military service. Some accepted noncombatant military service. Others accepted civilian alternative service. Still others refused to participate in any national ser-

A choir in an alternative service camp. (Photo: P.C. Tilitzky, in *That There be Peace*, p. 65)

vice. Others accepted civilian alternative service. Still others refused to participate in any national service program.

Most Mennonite and Brethren in Christ men participated in the civilian based alternative service program. In many respects this civilian program was highly successful. Much of the work cannot be quantified but nearly 11,000 men, including 7,500 Mennonites, participated.Over twenty million trees were planted in British Columbia alone. Innumerable forest fires were fought. Indeed, when the C.O.s were withdrawn from the B.C. Forestry Service, a newspaper wrote that it was losing "the most effective fire fighting service it has ever had." A federal Minister stated that "excellent service has been rendered by these conscientious objectors. They are, in the main, Mennonites, farmers' sons, well used to hard work." The money that they gave to the Red Cross, under the 1943 diversification arrangements, exceeded two million dollars.

In spite of this impressive work record, it was a difficult time. Being a C.O. was not popular in Canadian society. Still, many alternative service workers saw the program as their opportunity to serve their country in time of need without violating their religious teachings. It also brought them into contact with people of other backgrounds. This led some to probe their own beliefs more deeply. Not all were sincere. Several hundred volunteered for military service after working in the alternative service program for a time.

Some individuals feel that their alternative service has had a lasting effect on their lives. Gerhard Ens, who worked for nearly three years at what was then called the Manitoba School for Mentally Defective Persons in Portage La Prairie, writes: "I learned...about the whole area of mental retardation which has given me a great many insights for later years. I learned to be very thankful for my own health...."[21] David Schroeder who worked as an orderly at the St. Boniface Hospital in Winnipeg, Manitoba, writes: "most meaningful was the work with the patients themselves. You were with them during a time of difficulty in their life and they appreciated any help that you could give...it brought involvements with families. It was a ministry to people."[22] Vernon Toews, who completed a four-month alternative service assignment in a camp near Banff, Alberta, and then worked for two years under Mennonite Central Committee with children's homes in England and France, writes:

> ... many young men ... did not take the question of being a C.O. lightly. It caused many of us to come to terms with life, with their purpose in life, with the ultimate realities of existence, and possibly most important of all, with their relations with God.... The experience contributed vastly to my faith in Christ's gospel of love and salvation.... it made me want to make a positive contribution to mankind. The great question of the meaning of life and the purpose of existence was answered for me personally. I vaguely realized that God had put me into this world to help others— to love my neighbours as myself— and the first step in realizing this moral precept was my involvement with Mennonite Central Committee.[23]

For Canadian Mennonite and Brethren in Christ people generally, the war experience, was difficult, even divisive. But in the long run it contributed to a deeper service commitment and to greater unity. Late in the 1940s and 1950s, when another war seemed distinctly possible, some of the earlier differences were overcome and the various groups organized themselves in a more unified way so as to be better prepared in the event of another war and to be more diligent in alleviating human need even if another war did not come.

A home away from home. (Photo: Korny Wiens and H.P. Giesbrecht, in *That There be Peace*, p. 70.)

NOTES FOR THE FOREWORD

1. The number of deaths in the world comes from Ruth Leger Sivard, *World Military and Social Expenditures 1985*, published by World Priorities, Box 25140, Washington, D.C., 20007, p.11. The number of Canadian deaths was provided by security officials responsible for the Memorial Chapel, House of Commons, Ottawa. Their exact number is 44,893. Other sources say that only 39,000 Canadian service personnel died in World War II.

2. D.J. Nickel, in a memorandum sent to Mennonite Central Committee Canada (MCCC), April, 1988.

3. H.C. Born, in a letter to MCCC, April 7, 1988.

4. Frank Peters, "Hinter dem Gefaengnisgitter," *Mennonitische Welt*, November 1950. Also informative was a November 1989 telephone interview by William Janzen with Mrs. Margaret Peters of Killarney, Manitoba. She is a sister of Frank Peters. Frank Peters died in 1986. His death also made his Ottawa files inaccessible to the public for twenty years.

5. John J. Bergen, "Teaching Certificate is lost as Mennonite teacher maintains conscientious principles," *Mennonite Mirror*, XVIII, No. 5, January 1990, p.20.

6. Telephone interview by William Janzen with Gerhard Ens, Winnipeg, February 21, 1990.

SOURCES FOR PART I

For the sake of smoothness in reading we have not used "end notes" in Part I. However, a few words about sources are needed. The main source is Sam Martin himself. In 1983, at the request of Frances Greaser, he recorded his recollections on a tape. William Janzen conducted a number of shorter interviews with Mr. Martin in 1988 and 1989. A second important source is the Personal Records File, obtained from the National Archives of Canada and identified as National Defense Headquarters File #HQ 869-M-7296 Adm 3(a)2. Access to this file was obtained only after Sam Martin provided the necessary authorization. (Nearly all of the information in the SIGNIFICANT DATES section, PP.35-37, comes from this file.) A third source is file XV-11.4.9 at the Conrad Grebel College Archives in Waterloo, Ontario. It holds extensive documentation from the Conference of Historic Peace Churches. A fourth source are the B.B. Janz Papers, Vol. 42, in the Archives at the Mennonite Brethren Bible College in Winnipeg.

NOTES FOR PART II

1. William Janzen, *Limits on Liberty: The Experience of Mennonite, Hutterite and Doukhobor Communities in Canada*, Toronto, University of Toronto Press, 1990.

2. For a published summary of the World War I experience see Frank H. Epp, *Mennonites in Canada, 1786-1920: The History of a Separate People*, Toronto, Macmillan of Canada, 1974.

3. E.J. Swalm, *Nonresistance Under Test*, Nappanee, Indiana, E.V. Publishing House, first printing 1938, fourth printing 1952.

4. "Petition to His Excellency, the Governor-General of Canada in Council", November 4, 1918, signed by J.E. Doerr, the Solicitor for the Mennonites, National Archives of Canada (NA), R.G. 2,3. Vol.199. P.C. #2897.

5. Thomas P. Socknat, *Witness Against War: Pacifism in Canada 1900-1945*, Toronto, University of Toronto Press, 1987, p. 82ff and M. James Penton, *Jehovah's Witnesses in Canada: Champions of Freedom of Speech and Worship*, Toronto, Macmillan of Canada, 1976, p. 56ff.

6. Frank H. Epp, *Mennonite Exodus: The Rescue and Resettlement of the Russian Mennonites Since the Communist Revolution*, Altona, Manitoba, D.W. Friesen & Sons Ltd., 1962.

7. An important source on "Kanadier" activities is David P. Reimer, *Experience of the Mennonites in Canada during World War II*, (Steinbach, Manitoba, n.d.).

8. David Fransen, "As Far As Conscience Will Allow: Mennonites in Canada during the Second World War", *On Guard for Thee: War, Ethnicity and the Canadian State, 1939-1945*. ed. Norman Hillmer, et.al., Ottawa, published by Minister of Supply and Services Canada, 1988, p.131. See also David Fransen, "Canadian Mennonites and Conscientious Objection in World War II", and M.A. thesis in history, University of Waterloo, Waterloo, Ontario, 1977

9. Fransen, "As Far As Conscience Will Allow," . p.139,

10 J.A. Toews, *Alternative Service in Canada During World War II*, published by the Canadian Conference of the Mennonite Brethren Church, Winnipeg, 1959.

11. Letter. J.F.L. Embury to Walter Tucker, M.P., January 12, 1942, NA, R.G. 27. Vol.986, file 1.

12. Letter. David Toews to F.C. Blair, July 13, 1942, Canadian Mennonite Heritage Centre Archives, (CMHCA), Vol.1322, Vol.930.

13. Letter, David Toews to J.T. Thorson, July 14, 1942, Ibid.

14. Letter, David Toews and C.F.Klassen, to J.T. Thorson, September 28, 1942, NA, R.G. 27. Vol. 991, file 2-101-1.

15. Ken Reddig, "Manitoba Mennonites and the Winnipeg Mobilization Board in World War II," an M.A. thesis in history, University of Manitoba, Winnipeg, Manitoba, 1989, p. 109.

16. N.N. Driedger, *The Leamington United Mennonite Church: Establishment and Development 1925-1972.* Printed by D.W. Friesen & Sons Ltd., Altona, Manitoba, 1972, p. 71.

17. Socknat, op. cit., p. 250ff.

18. Statement of Doukhbour Delegation (Union of Spiritual Community of Christ), November 16, 1943, NA, R.G. 27, Vol. 991, file 2-101-2, part 2.

19. Letter, S.T.Wood to Louis St. Laurent, March 15, 1944, NA, R.G. 27, Vol. 133, file 601. 3-6-1 (Vol.4).

20. Fransen, op. cit.

21. As quoted in Lawrence Klippenstein (ed.), *That There Be Peace: Mennonites in Canada and World War II*, The Manitoba CO Reunion Committee, Winnipeg, 1979.

22. Ibid.

23. Vernon K. Toews, "I was a C.O. in World War II," in *Manitoba Mennonite Memories 1874-1974* (ed.) Julius G. Toews and Lawrence Klippenstein, Manitoba Mennonite Centennial Committee, Altona, Manitoba, 1974.